MW01060354

SELF-CARE IN UNDERWEAR

SELF-CARE IN UNDERWEAR

YOGA IN YOUR UNDIES, BUBBLE BATHS, AND 50+ MORE WAYS TO IMPROVE WELL-BEING

BY TON MAK

CHRONICLE BOOKS

SAN FRANCISCO

Copyright © 2022 by Ton Mak.

All rights reserved. No part of this book may be reproduced in
any form without written permission from the publisher.

Library of Congress Cataloging-in-Publication Data available.

ISBN 978-1-7972-1421-4

Manufactured in China.

Design by Rachel Harrell.
Authenticity read by Jay Justice.

Typeset in Bryant.

Airstream is a registered trademark of Thor Tech, Inc.; Instagram is
a registered trademark of Instagram, LLC; Wikipedia is a registered
trademark of Wikimedia Foundation, Inc.; YouTube is a registered
trademark of Google, LLC.

10 9 8 7 6 5 4 3 2 1

Chronicle books and gifts are available at special quantity
discounts to corporations, professional associations, literacy
programs, and other organizations. For details and discount
information, please contact our premiums department at
corporatesales@chroniclebooks.com or at 1-800-759-0190.

Chronicle Books LLC
680 Second Street
San Francisco, California 94107
www.chroniclebooks.com

This book is dedicated to my no. 1
self-care-inspiration and best pal, Anmao.

TAKE GOOD CARE OF YOUR GOOD SELF

Self-care is soothing nourishment for your mind, heart, and body. It should feel accessible and comforting, like melted peanut butter on toasted bread.

In moments of "meh" and "bleh," having a nifty personal tool kit of self-care practices and habits can help you find a sense of calm. It can restore balance and remind you to be kinder to yourself.

Self-care doesn't have to be luxurious, involve pampering, or require much work at all. It can be as simple as pausing for a moment, returning to the sofa, and enjoying a puff pastry with a fluffy friend. Day to day, there are tiny practices that can help you navigate all your oscillating emotions. And some days, perhaps the most productive thing you can do is nothing at all.

HEllO PANSY

Meet Pansy. Affectionately known as No-Pants Pansy.

She's a wholesome gal who loves to live life in maximum comfort—in her many pairs of underpants.

Whether she is alone, with her pals, or with her fluffy animal friends, Pansy makes time for small pleasures and delights.

Here, our friend Pansy shares some of her favorite ways to unwind—sans pants, of course. Simply flip to any page to uncover easy-peasy, pick-me-up practices that can help you recharge and relax.

LOVE ME A GOOD ROUTINE

We all have little rituals and routines to call our own. A series of repetitive behaviors that serve a purpose, routines give us a sense of control thanks to their predictable and comforting nature.

Whether it is welcoming each day, writing out your to-do list, or brewing your tea, everyday actions treated with care and attention can be transformed into nourishing moments of self-care.

For Pansy, each morning kicks off with her staring into space while enjoying a bowl of fibrous cereal.

Treat yourself to plenty of good sleep. Hit snooze and wiggle in bed a little longer if need be.

WONDERFUL MORNI

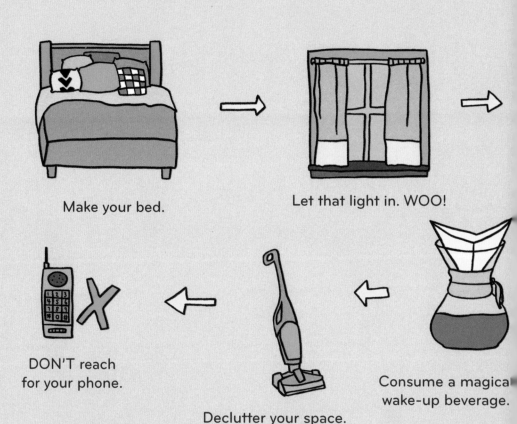

Make your bed.

Let that light in. WOO!

Consume a magica
wake-up beverage.

Declutter your space.

DON'T reach
for your phone.

NG ROUTINE :

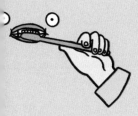

Clean your face
and brush your teeth.

Drink a glass
of water.

TO DO:
1. ___
2. ___
3. ___
4. ___

Set some goals
for the day.

Do some morning
stretches.

Take a mindful moment as you brew
your first cup of the day.

Keep a gratitude journal, and jot down every day's greatest hits and inspirations.

Give thanks to your cat.

DAILY ☼ MORNING JOURNAL PROMPTS

3 things I am grateful for

3 things that I want to feel today

3 things I can do to make today a good day

DAILY AFFIRMATIONS :

1. I am enough.
2. I make delicious muffins.
3. My skin is decently smooth.
4. I am a thoughtful nugget.

SMALL THINGS TO BE THANKFUL ♥FOR♥:

A world full of diversity

A comfy bed

A healthy plant

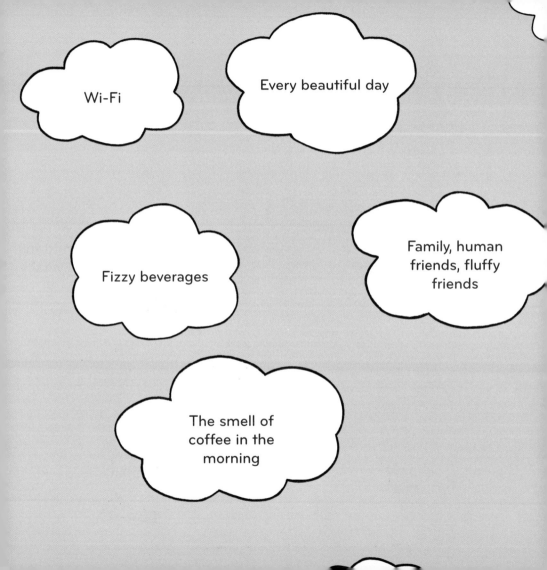

Roll out the yoga mat. Have a sit. Stretch
the stresses away.

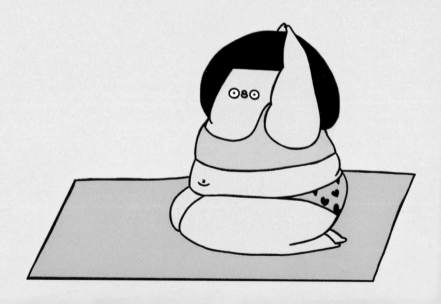

Foam roll, jade roll, just . . . roll.

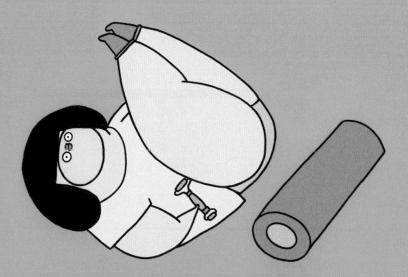

Get moving! Be active, whatever that means to you: Go on a walk, do some stretches, or if you're feeling extra, experiment with crow pose.

Stay hydrated. Always and forever.

COZY + RELA
BEDTIME

Turn up the relaxing vibes:
dim the lights and light a candle.

Take a warm and
pampering bath.

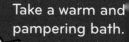

Get snuggled up
nice and cozy.

Take a moment to
reflect on your day:
meditate, pray, or
journal.

XING + FUZZY ROUTINE

Make a soothing cup of herbal tea.

Do some nighttime stretches.

Unplug and enjoy some tech-free time.

THE ART OF THE RECHARGE

There will always be those overwhelming days where you really just want to hit the reboot button.

We all have our interpretations of what it means to "recharge" and what is restful. For some, it could be cocooning in a corner in deep silence, whilst for others, it could be an intense marathon-style run with like-minded buddies. For Pansy, recharging means being horizontal, snacking on rice crackers, and communing with a few fluffy pals.

Our bodies are hardwired to help us cope and heal in our own unique ways; the key is simply knowing when to pause and which boosters work best for you.

ARIES
Camp out in an
Airstream in the
wilderness for
a few days.

LEO
Get dressed
up and go on
a solo date.

GEMINI
Write a
lengthy life
story to a
friend via text.

TAURUS
Indulge in
YouTube content,
with your laptop
gently warming
on your chest.

CANCER
Go down a
Wikipedia rabbit
hole of largely
underwhelming
historical figures.

VIRGO
Follow a strict
itinerary of perfectly
curated relaxing
activities.

RECHARGE
TROLOGICAL SIGN: ⚡

CAPRICORN
Binge-watch "Survival Skills to Know" videos on the internet.

SAGITTARIUS
Decide in the moment whatever feels right.

LIBRA
int watercolor portraits of Instagram-nous animals.

PISCES
Stare out the window and reminisce about a meal from 2001.

SCORPIO
Hibernate with a dystopian novel in n artfully scented atmosphere.

AQUARIUS
Submerge yourself in ambient noise.

Meditate.

Enjoy a slice of silence.

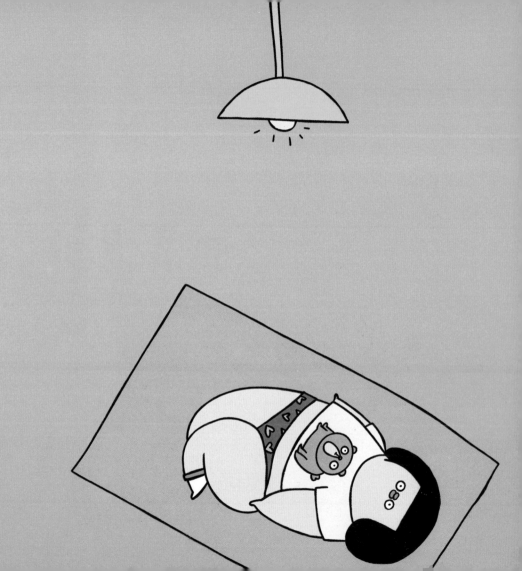

Go on a picnic with a fine and elegant display of treats.

Picnic blanket

Fancy cutlery

Paper napkins

Beige-colored foods

Bubbly beverages

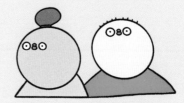

Pals

A ball to encourage engagement

Lovingly sliced fruits

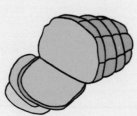

Ham(s)

A book to encourage disengagement

SHOULD I HAVE A

ARE YOU HUNGRY?

Yes.

Unsure . . . meh.

Look, it's been rough

HAVE A SNACK!!!

SNACK ?

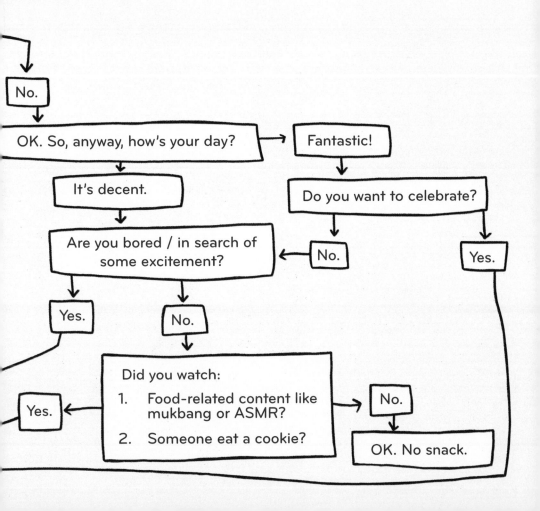

No.

OK. So, anyway, how's your day? → Fantastic!

It's decent.

Do you want to celebrate?

Are you bored / in search of some excitement? ← No.

Yes.

Yes.

No.

Did you watch:

1. Food-related content like mukbang or ASMR?

2. Someone eat a cookie?

→ No.

Yes.

OK. No snack.

Reconnect with nature.

Admire the sky. Think about your neighbor's dog.

Enjoy a good conversation with family and pals.

If there is an awkward silence, just smile warmly for an extended period of time.

SHOULD I TAKE A NA

IS IT THE WEEKEND?

Yes.

No.

Did you stay up late last night?

Yes.

No.

Do you feel lethargic or not-in-a-good-way funky?

Yes.

No.

Ye

TAKE A NAP!!!

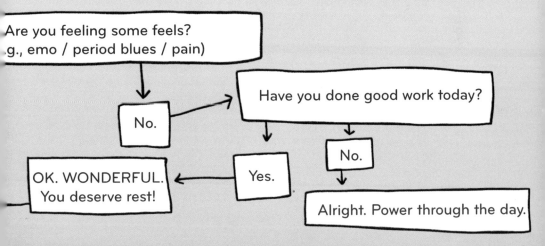

Schedule an at-home spa day. Invite the pals and meditatively watch their pet(s) in silence.

Retire to the sofa for a good old
inhale-exhale.

Roll yourself into a warm burrito.

CLEAN UP + GLOW UP

The spaces we live and work in have plenty of influence on our mental well-being. By maintaining outer order, we can create inner harmony (cliché, but true). It could be as simple as throwing out expired cheese, making your bed, making your dog's bed, or reorganizing your snack selection.

Once you notice how lovely it feels to keep things clean, it will seem much less like a chore and more like an act of self-love.

Oh, and the same applies to cleaning yourself. From enjoying a simple face wash in the morning to indulging in a more luxurious body scrub, these micro-moments of nourishment all add up, making us feel nice and shiny.

Declutter and make space for fresh thoughts.

Do a deep clean every now and then.

Be sure to feel proud of yourself afterward.

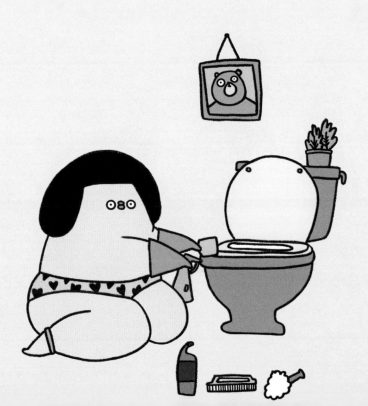

Keep tabs on the fullness of your fridge.

You never know what's hiding in there.

Rearrange your closet, and hopefully locate your missing cat.

Enjoy a good laundry day.

Then, face-plant into your warm, freshly clean clothes.

STUFF THAT YOU CA[N]
FOR A BETTER SENSE

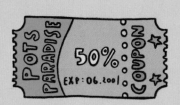

Expired coupons

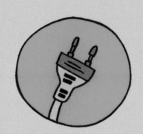

Unidentifiable cables for
ancient technology

Clothes that could go
to better places

Very old
to-do lists

PERHAPS CLEAR OUT OF WELL-BEING:

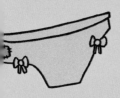

Very very very
old underwear

Magazines
from 1997

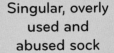

Singular, overly
used and
abused sock

Stacks of business cards for
the job you left a decade ago

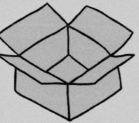

Suspiciously clean
delivery boxes

Buy containers.

Feel proud.

Take a very, very long bath.

Moisturize in slow motion.

THE PERFECT BUBBLE BATH TO SOAK YOUR WOES AWAY:

❀ Make time.

❀ Switch on "do not disturb" mode.

❀ Dim the lights and light a candle for vibes.

❀ Add an invigorating bath bomb or healing bath salts to perfectly warm water.

❀ Apply a face mask to maximize this relaxing moment.

❀ Sip on herbal tea.

❀ Take a deep breath and sink into the suds.

❀ Enjoy a show, movie, book, or slice of leftover pizza.

HOME SWEET HOME

One of the most cozy of all words is "home." There is something soothing about going nowhere and simply being in the comforts of your humble dwelling. There is no better place to meditate, develop new hobbies, revisit old comforts, and just be in stretchy pants—or, if you're like Pansy, in no pants at all.

Turn up the mood lighting when the time is right.

Master a soup-for-the-soul recipe. This will come in handy, especially in times of low energy or cold feet (physically or mentally).

Cook a wholesome adult meal for yourself.

Pair it with sparkling water in a fancy glass.

Find yourself a comfortable corner for a bit of me time.

Staring into space is a critically important activity.

Get completely lost in a riveting read.

Look after a houseplant. Try not to let it die.

Peace, love, and plants.

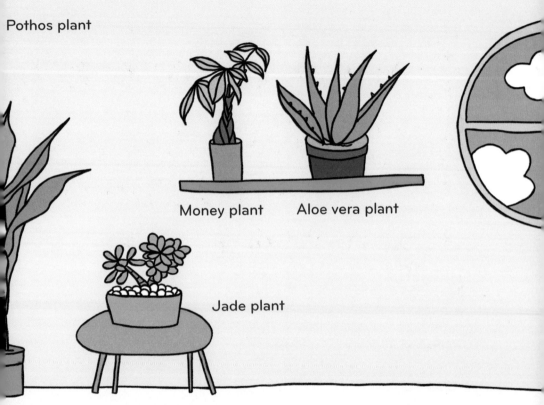

Pothos plant

Money plant

Aloe vera plant

Jade plant

Cast-iron
plant

Treat yourself to some fresh flowers.

Envision yourself as the protagonist in a classic English novel as you walk home with an elegant bunch.

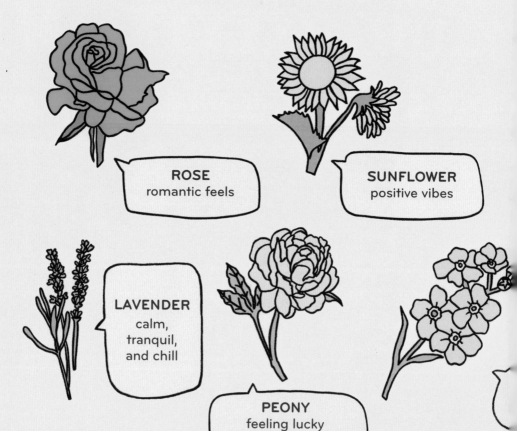

ROSE
romantic feels

SUNFLOWER
positive vibes

LAVENDER
calm,
tranquil,
and chill

PEONY
feeling lucky

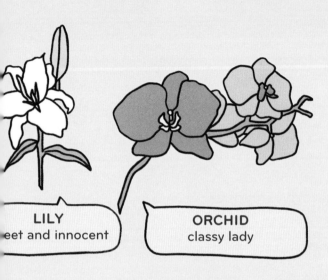

Explore some wholesome hobbies.

Knit a cardigan for your favorite mug.

Get lost in an ambitious puzzle.

THE LITTLE THINGS

Sometimes, the smallest things bring us the most joy—noticing a new succulent on your daily walk, waking up to the smell of coffee beans, or treating yourself to an unusual scented candle.

By being fully present when soaking up all the small pleasures in life, or by simply being a more attentive doer and listener, you can turn a single moment into much, much more. Even a quiet morning with your favorite pastry can become an especially memorable instant in time when you give it your fullest attention.

Pump up some jams to suit the mood.

Let the thought of being the lead in that very music video take you far, far away.

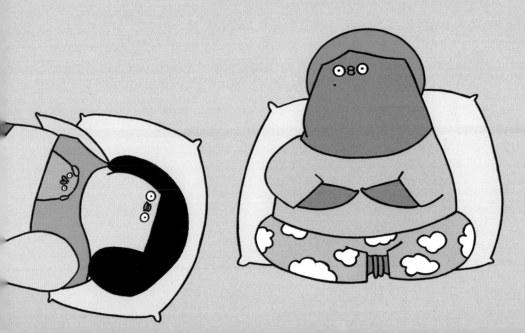

Treat yourself to a warm beverage . . .

and other coffee shop delights. Any
day is an excellent day for a pastry.

ROOIBOS

Ultimate calming nap time companion

Supports heart health ♥

PEPPERMINT

Digestive aid full of antioxidants ~ poop your worries away

Soothing calm, for anytime

GREEN

The immune system's BFF ~ say bye-bye to nausea

Mood and energy booster ~ packed full of antioxidants

LEMON BALM

Visit a local bookstore and smell some books.

Play with fluffy friends.

You may acknowledge them before you acknowledge their respective owners, and that's OK.

Procrastibake.

Have a get-together with some friends and all your favorite party foods . . .

A potluck perhaps.

People-watch in a socially acceptable and non-creepy manner.

Indulge in animal-related memes.

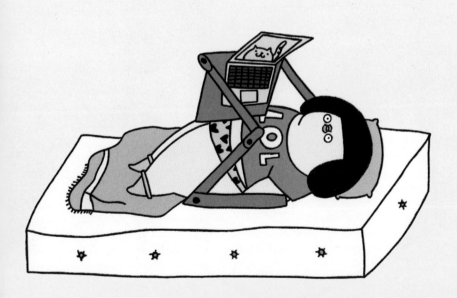

Sit by the fan or AC on a summer day. Let it blast your face with coolness.

Go on an adventure with your favorite pal. The grocery store can be an exciting place too!

Get pleasantly lost exploring new hiking trails. Roar, bark, yell, or meow when you reach the top of a hill.

Enjoy some art and the peace that comes from just looking (or from being utterly confused).

Take a mindful walk around the neighborhood.

Try not to gaze too intensely into people's homes.

Go on an adventure in the woods. Maybe you will feel mildly
anxious about the unpredictable wildlife, and that's OK.

Write down your feels, dreams, or to-do lists.
Having all your thoughts written out can be a relief.

Air out your dirty laundry.

BE KIND TO YOUR WONDERFUL SELF

Last but not least, self-care is about being a more supportive and kind friend to yourself. There are days when you hold yourself to all sorts of expectations or self-judgments; you want to keep everything in control. But your inner cheerleader deserves your attention too! Sometimes, you just need to take a break and remind yourself that even if you don't achieve the perfection that you demand, you are good enough; you are excellent.

So, let's all give ourselves a thumbs-up and a 5-star review. And remember . . .

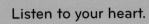
Listen to your heart.

Say "NAH!" when you need to.

Enjoy a slow-motion lifestyle.

Give yourself plenty of encouragement . . .

and a big, big hug.

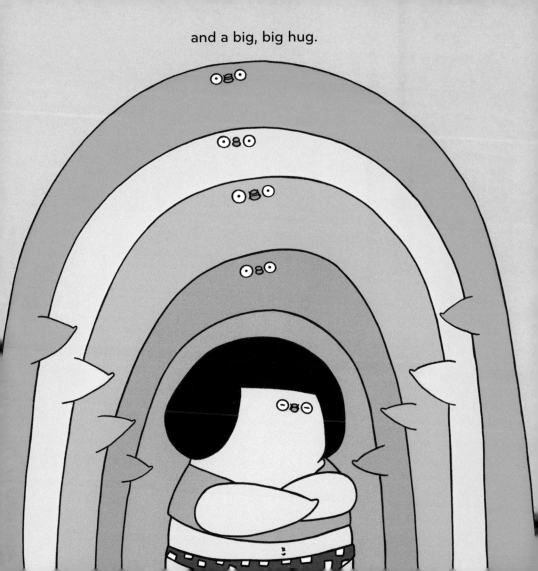

ACKNOWLEDGMENTS

A big thank you to Claire Gilhuly from Chronicle Books for showing love and support for Pansy from the get-go. I'd also like to thank Monika Verma for being a wonderful guardian to Pansy along the way.

ABOUT THE AUTHOR

Ton Mak is a visual artist and writer. Her specialty lies in a series of bouncy, friendly, and often chubby creatures known as FLABJACKS. Ton is the author of *A Sloth's Guide to Mindfulness* and *A Turtle's Guide to Introversion*. She likes hot tea, chicken broth, and potato chips. Currently, Ton splits her time between San Francisco and Shanghai.

For more happy happenings, visit www.flabjacks.com.